# A Proper Newe Booke of Cokerye

# A Proper Newe Booke of Cokerye

*Margaret Parker's Cookery Book*

EDITED BY ANNE AHMED

Illustrated by Chihiro Mizuta

Facsimile by John Cleaver

CORPUS CHRISTI COLLEGE
CAMBRIDGE

© Corpus Christi College 2002
Published by Corpus Christi College, Cambridge CB2 1RH

All rights reserved. No part of this publication may be reproduced, stored in any retrieval system or transmitted in any form or by any means, electronic, mechanical, photocopying, recording or otherwise, without the prior permission of the publishers.

A CIP catalogue record of this book is available from the British Library

ISBN 0 9504261 3 X

Designed by Tim McPhee
Production Services by Book Production Consultants plc,
25–27 High Street, Chesterton, Cambridge CB4 1ND

Printed and bound by The Wolsey Press, Ipswich

The front cover shows a drawing of Lambeth Palace based on the Hollar print held at Lambeth Palace Library and the Old Court, Corpus Christi College, Cambridge.

# Contents

| | |
|---|---|
| Foreword by Christopher de Hamel | vii |
| Preface | xi |
| Acknowledgements | xiii |
| Introduction | 1 |
| Facsimile of text with interpretation | 23 |
| Recipes | 83 |
| Bibliography | 98 |

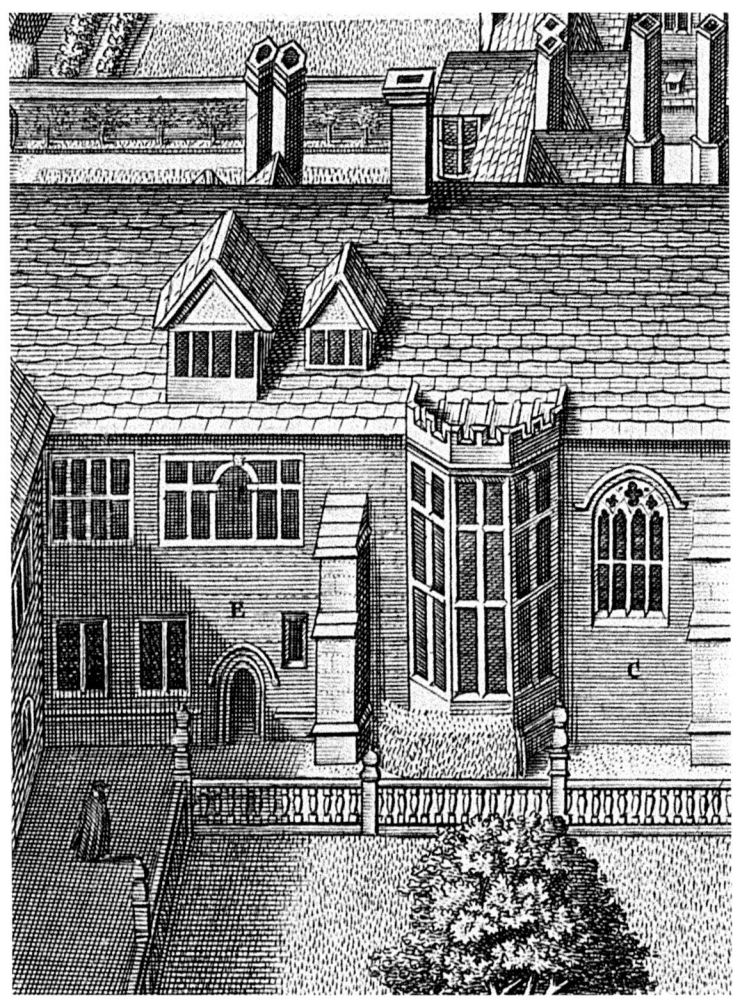

*The old medieval Master's Lodge, Corpus Christi College. Detail from D. Loggan,* Cantabrigia Illustrata, *1690.*

# Foreword

Corpus Christi College is one of the medieval foundations that make up the University of Cambridge. Visitors to the College enter now through a great neo-gothic gateway into a vast early-nineteenth-century courtyard. Almost directly opposite the gate is the Master's Lodge, the imposing residence of the Master of the College, who presides over its fifty or so Fellows and about four hundred students who are members of the College. Along the right-hand side of the courtyard, adjoining the corner of the Master's Lodge, is the Parker Library, one of the finest and most perfectly preserved small collections of early books and manuscripts in England. The core of the library was entrusted to the care of the College in 1574 by Archbishop Matthew Parker (1504–75), its fourteenth Master.

Parker was a passionate book collector, interested in history, language, theology, travel and many other subjects. The library's medieval manuscripts include some of the most important Anglo-Saxon books in existence. It is generally, however, a very serious and highbrow collection, with very little in the way of frivolous material, such as literature or Latin classics. One of the most unlikely books in such a collection, put together by an archbishop, is a little practical textbook on cookery. In any context

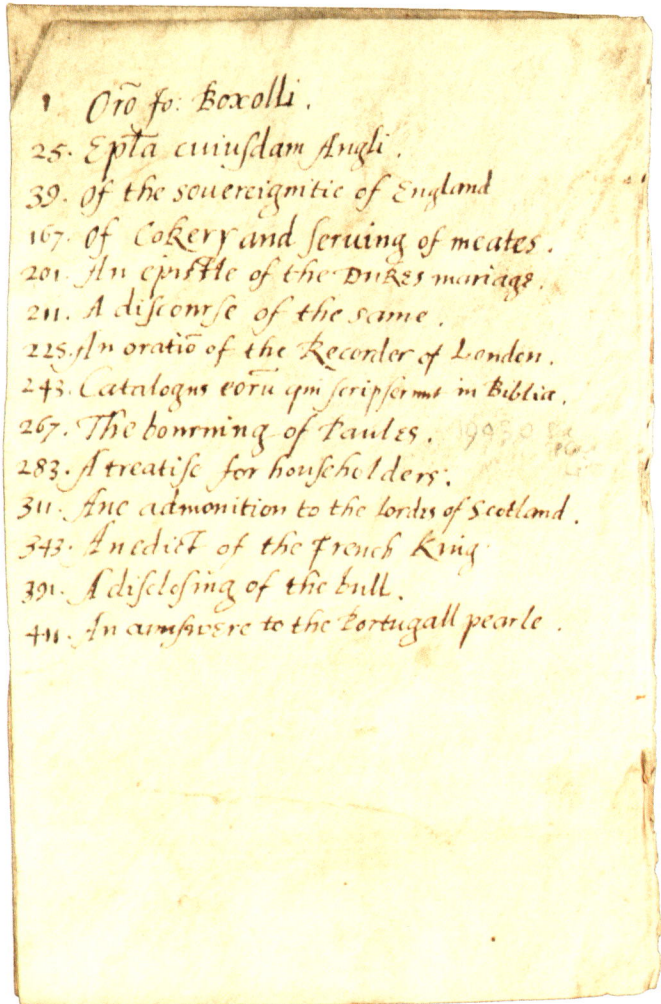

*Contents of the bound volume, including the cookbook, written by Matthew Parker in his own hand.*

such books are extraordinarily rare. It is a volume intended for daily use. Tudor cookery books, like their counterparts today, were used in kitchens in close proximity to food and liquids; they were often handled hurriedly and they were quite literally used to pieces. To judge from what we know of the printer, the cookbook in the Parker Library was published in 1557–8. No other copy of this edition is known to survive.

The book is preserved bound up into a collection of short texts assembled and indexed by Matthew Parker himself. The whole volume consists of fourteen little tracts bound together in covers of sixteenth-century white vellum with soft leather ties. The other texts are all concerned with political or religious topics. The book on cooking is sandwiched between a booklet on the claims of the kings of England to the sovereignty of Scotland (1548) and a letter on the imprisonment of the Duke of Norfolk (1571). It seems such an unlikely book for the theological and political library of an archbishop that it is commonly supposed that it must have belonged to Margaret Parker, Matthew's wife, who was known in her lifetime for hospitality and entertainment. The date of publication, 1557–8, corresponds precisely to the period when Matthew Parker and his wife were living together, probably in relative domestic simplicity, after being expelled from Corpus under Queen Mary – just before his appointment to Canterbury. Later there would have been many domestic servants at Lambeth Palace and Margaret Parker would hardly have been required in the kitchens. The little book from their period of exile was doubtless swept up among the family's books brought down to Lambeth, still in excellent condition for it was then only a year or so old. After Margaret's death, it was bound up by the

Archbishop into the composite volume in which it still survives. Matthew Parker himself wrote a list of contents, describing it as being 'On Cokery and serving of meates'.

The present Master of Corpus Christi College, Professor Haroon Ahmed, is also a book collector. It is particularly appropriate that his wife, Anne Ahmed, should have been persuaded to prepare the present edition of the volume popularly known as 'Mrs Parker's Cookbook' because Mrs Ahmed herself, stands in a direct and unbroken line of succession from Margaret Parker. It offers a rare and fascinating glimpse into sixteenth-century domestic life. The facsimile is published in the 650th anniversary year of a College in which both Mrs Parker and Mrs Ahmed have occupied the Master's Lodge.

Christopher de Hamel
Donnelley Fellow Librarian

# Preface

This book has been published to commemorate the 650th anniversary of the founding of Corpus Christi College in Cambridge. *A Proper Newe Booke of Cokerye* forms part of the Parker Library and could well have been used by Matthew Parker's wife Margaret in the sixteenth century.

The introduction describes the life and times of Matthew and Margaret Parker. In writing this introduction, I found myself relating a fascinating story of love and constancy through momentous times in Tudor England. This story helps perhaps to explain why, among the many historical books and papers of Church and State that Matthew Parker bequeathed to Corpus Christi College, he included this little book with its link to his beloved wife.

In this edition a facsimile of the cookbook has been reproduced, together with an interpretation based on the notes accompanying the scholarly edition of *A Proper Newe Booke of Cokerye* edited by Catherine Frances Frere and published in 1913.

The facsimile was produced by digitising the original pages after removing them from the binding. The high resolution of the digitisation process at 1200 pixels per inch and subsequent computer-aided processing of the images have made it possible to produce a faithful reproduction of text, colour and size. The plate showing the Master's Lodge in the Old Court at the time of Margaret Parker's residence is an enlargement of a small portion of the engraving of the College by Loggan, which also was digitised.

The line drawings which illustrate the recipes were chosen to reflect life in Margaret Parker's time. The front cover shows the Parkers' two main residences in Corpus Christi College and Lambeth.

I have also included in this edition modern versions of some of the recipes from the cookbook. These have been tried out informally and adapted for today's cooks. Although most of the ingredients used in Margaret Parker's time are still available, the recipes have been modified for convenience. Readers may wish to interpret and develop these recipes in different ways. It has been an interesting experience to prepare and serve some of these dishes while entertaining in the Master's Lodge.

I hope that readers will enjoy this book not only for its unusual recipes but also for its association with Corpus Christi College in Cambridge.

Anne Ahmed<br>
March 2002

# Acknowledgements

In undertaking the task of producing this edition, I have been helped considerably by a number of people. Angie Cole prepared some of the recipes and helped with the interpretation of the facsimile. Betty Bury, Ayesha Ahmed, Angie Cole and Tim Cole read the text and gave helpful advice. Gill Cannell, Sub-Librarian of the Parker Library, helped me with her considerable expertise in seeking reference material. Oliver Rackham read the introduction for historical accuracy, Catherine Hall, Library Archivist, identified and translated the page of Corpus Christi College accounts and many others were encouraging and supportive.

The project was supported by a generous donation given by the Worshipful Company of Cooks of London who provided part of the publication costs. Finally, I should like to thank the Master and Fellows of Corpus Christi College for their support of this project.

Anne Ahmed

*The pelican has formed part of the coat of arms of Corpus Christi College since Matthew Parker's Mastership* (From a drawing by A.T Clarke, 1981)

# Introduction

Matthew Parker was Master of Corpus Christi College in Cambridge from 1544 to 1553 and Archbishop of Canterbury from 1559 to 1575. Amongst the books and papers which he bequeathed to the College is a small book which contains, among other material within its binding, a volume entitled *A Proper Newe Booke of Cokerye*. This, it is reasonable to suppose, had at one time been used by his wife Margaret. This particular edition was probably printed in 1557–8 and is the only known copy of that printing. There is an earlier edition dated 1545 at the University of Glasgow and two later editions in the British Library. Cookery books in the sixteenth century were often collections of recipes and suggestions passed on from one household to another, and were not as structured as those produced today. *A Proper Newe Booke of Cokerye* includes within its pages lists of meat and fish together with suggestions for specific sauces. The recipes in the book do not contain detailed instructions for preparation or cooking.

Margaret, the supposed owner of the book, was the daughter of Robert Harleston, gentleman, and was born into a Norfolk family almost 500 years ago. She grew up to become the wife of the fourteenth Master of Corpus Christi College, who was later the first Archbishop of Canterbury to be consecrated in the reign of Queen Elizabeth I. Corpus Christi College was founded in 1352 and it was customary for Masters of the College to be ordained priests. As a consequence of her marriage Margaret became not only the first wife to live in Corpus Christi College, but probably also the first to live in Lambeth Palace. The momentous changes which took place in both Church and State during her lifetime give her a unique place in English social history.

Margaret came from a well-established family. Despite losing her mother at an early age, she must have been brought up with love and care; Strype who wrote a biography of Matthew Parker, called her 'accomplished in all good endowments both of body and mind.'[1] Born in 1519, she had been well educated like many women of her class. As the only daughter of a widower, she would have been involved in the running of her father's household, taking responsibility for supervising the provision of food and drink. In the sixteenth century the education of girls, regardless of social position, included lessons on domestic aspects of life, since as married women they would be expected to see that their households were fed and clothed, and as far as possible kept in good health. Decorous behaviour was expected, and girls were brought up to be chaste, silent, and obedient to their husbands.

Matthew Parker was born in the early years of the sixteenth century, also in Norfolk. He was admitted to Corpus Christi College in 1521 and obtained his BA in 1524, was ordained priest in 1527 and became a Fellow of the College in 1528. In 1544 Henry VIII, whose chaplain he had been, commended him as

---

1. J. Strype, *The Life and Acts of Matthew Parker*...1711, Book 1, page 24.

*A sixteenth-century feast from* Navis Stultifera *by Sebastian Brant, published in 1505 in Paris.*

Master to the Fellows of Corpus and he was elected later that year. By this time he and Margaret, in circumstances that are not recorded, had already met and come to an understanding. Clerical marriage had died out by the early Middle Ages, and since both Church and State forbade the marriage of priests, Matthew and Margaret agreed to take no other partner, but to remain faithful to one another. Margaret would have been aware that the marriage of someone in holy orders was a breach of the priest's rule of celibacy and chastity. Strype comments that they were 'dear to one another but abstained from wedlock by mutual agreement'.[2]

In 1547 Henry VIII died and was succeeded by Edward VI. One outcome of this change, together with the continuing rise of Protestantism, meant that laws governing the marriage of priests were repealed, and this allowed Matthew and Margaret to marry. Margaret had waited for Matthew for seven years although she must have had many suitors during that period. In Tudor times to be unwed at 28 was very unusual for a woman. Matthew and Margaret were married in 1547, on the day after her twenty-eighth birthday. Matthew was 42. The wedding was a private affair and it is not known where it took place. Margaret came to live with Matthew as his wife in the Master's Lodge of Corpus Christi College, and her life was changed dramatically. It must have taken some courage to marry a clergyman in those days, especially one who was highly regarded and lived so very public a life. Clergy wives were not popular in society and were sometimes subjected to abuse by other married women. During his

2. Strype, Book 1, page 24.

Mastership, Matthew Parker was twice Vice-Chancellor and was involved at the highest level of Cambridge society.

Theirs was by all accounts a happy marriage, with Margaret maintaining a strong supportive role as her husband's career advanced. As Master, Matthew was heavily involved in College life, acting as Bursar, sorting out College accounts, increasing the benefits for students and creating studentships and Fellowships. He was intimate with many prominent people of his age, such as Nicholas Bacon and Nicholas Ridley, and with many leading reformers – Bilney, Barnes and Latimer among them. Margaret was certainly noticed by his friends and Ridley – who was a bachelor – when referring to her was reputed to have asked if she had a sister. Stokes, who wrote a history of Corpus Christi College, comments on Margaret's 'graceful rule in the Lodge' and her 'dignified hospitality'.[3] The Master's Lodge became famous for hospitality and the Parkers would have entertained many prominent people during their time at Corpus. Unlike now, it was not the norm then to entertain students or other Members of the College in the Master's Lodge.

While at Corpus Christi College, Matthew Parker improved and expanded the Master's Lodge which was then in the south-east corner of the Old Court of the College, adding a long gallery with an open walk beneath it and steps into the garden. Matthew loved gardens and had spent a great deal of time improving the garden at Stoke College in Suffolk before he came to Cambridge. Sadly, some of his improvements at Corpus have disappeared over time, especially with the building of the

---

3. H.P. Stokes, *Corpus Christi*, 1898, page 53.

*The account of the 1547 feast Corpus Christi College Muniments College Accounts II.2. Feasts 1517–1562.*

## Expenses made in the feast of Corpus Christi anno domini 1547 and of King Edward the sixth

| | |
|---|---:|
| In white bread | 3s |
| In bread for the poor | 12d |
| In best drink | 20d |
| In mixed drink | 18d |
| In beer (with hops) | 2s 8d |
| In fuel | 20d |
| | |
| In spices as shown in schedule | 10s 3½d |
| | |
| Item a busshell of flower and more | 17d |
| | |
| Item 4 pygges | 3s |
| Item 4 capons | 3s 6d |
| Item one other capon | 13d |
| Item a dosyng checkens | 23d |
| Item halfe a dosyng checkens | 10d |
| Item for 5 checkens | 8d |
| Item 6 geese | 2s 6d |
| Item for a calfe | 4s 6d |
| Item for a shepe | 4s 8d |
| Item for a lamme | 2s |
| | |
| Item for a ....ter on Wednesday at nyg(t) | 12d |
| Item for 4 legges of mutton | 16d |

*Translated by Catherine Hall*

New Court in the early nineteenth century, when the present Master's Lodge was built.

Three of the Parkers' four children were born during their time at Corpus and one of them died there in infancy. Only two of the four children survived to adulthood. Infant mortality was very high in the sixteenth century and childbirth was a hazardous experience. Childbirth would have allowed Margaret to drop out of normal society for a while, taking to her chamber with female support until the baby was born. She would have reappeared eventually after a ritual period into society, following her participation in the service set out in the Prayer Book for the *Churching of Women*. This service continued in use in many parts of England until the mid-twentieth century. Their first son John was born in 1548. His godfather was John Mere, who was a benefactor both to the University and to the College. To this day a sermon is preached every year in St Bene't's Church in Mere's memory.

Although we know little about Margaret's daily life at that time, there is much information about a contemporary of hers who, although younger, was married in the same year to Sir William Cavendish. She was the redoubtable Bess of Hardwick, reputed to be a strong and independent woman. Some of Bess's children were born in similar years to Margaret's and two of them also died in infancy. When Margaret died, Bess had been married and widowed three times. Accounts of Bess's life give us a window into the style of life Margaret must have lived in Cambridge, London and Canterbury.

Life was happy for the Parker family in the Master's Lodge until Queen Mary came to the throne in 1553. She enforced the annulment of the Edwardian act of permission for priests to marry. Every married clergyman was to 'put away' his wife. All clergy had to follow her edicts. After waiting for so long to marry and experiencing a stable and happy lifestyle with Margaret, Matthew, who was now deeply attached to his wife, felt that he had no choice but to resign the Mastership and retire to live in obscurity in the country. He was deprived of his prebend in the church of Ely and of the rectory of Landbeach. He was despoiled of the deanery of Lincoln and prebend of Coringham. However he did enjoy 'delightful literary leisure'[4] during that time and no doubt the constant companionship of his beloved Margaret.

The Parkers must have missed their friends after leaving Cambridge, and would have been saddened by news of the dreadful fate of many of their associates – including Latimer, Ridley and Cranmer, who were martyred for their religious beliefs. During this period, according to Strype, Matthew Parker's exile was made easier by his 'good and chaste wife' and his 'two dear little sons'[5]. In 1556 another son was born, sadly, he died the same year. Matthew was not idle during this time. He took advantage of his enforced seclusion to translate the Psalms into metrical verse. He also wrote a book, *The Defence of the Marriage of Priests*, which was not published until 1562.

On Mary's death, her half-sister Elizabeth was released from the Tower of London and declared Queen of England. On her accession to the throne she asked Matthew Parker, who had been chaplain to her mother, Anne Boleyn, to become her first Archbishop of Canterbury. Matthew, Anne's exact contemporary

---

4. Strype, Book 1, page 32. Translated from Latin, from Matthew Parker's Parchment Roll.
5. *Ibid.*

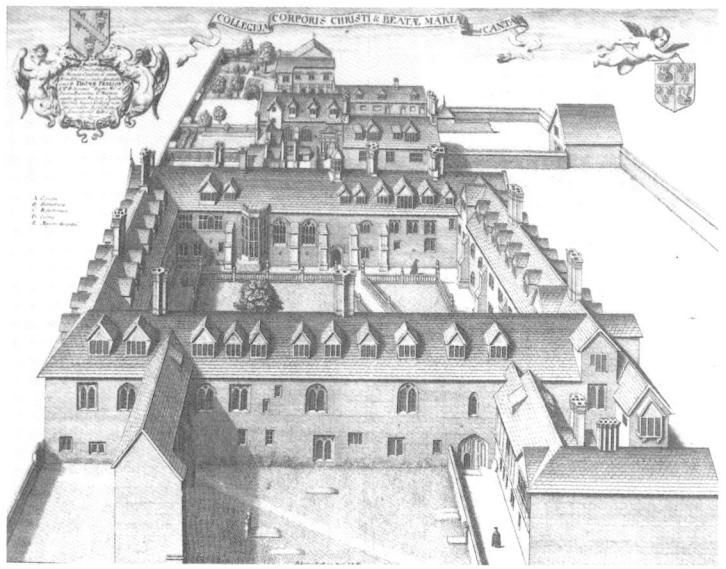

*Corpus Christi College from the north. From D. Loggan,* Cantabrigia Illustrata, *1690.*

in age, had been her faithful attendant from her first moments as Queen until her death by execution, when it is said that her blood was spattered on his clothing. Matthew was by now 55 years old and reluctant to take up the great office that he was being offered. He and Margaret and their two surviving sons were now settled comfortably back in Cambridge, and Elizabeth's views, disapproving of married clergy, were well known. He agreed eventually to take up office, and on 17 December 1559 he was consecrated Archbishop of Canterbury and moved with his wife and sons into Lambeth Palace.

Despite his immense new responsibilities, Matthew Parker

spent some of his time during his first years as Archbishop, furnishing his household at Lambeth and repairing the palace at Canterbury. In both these residences he established a reputation for hospitality. According to Strype, he wished to 'receive both the clergy and gentry with the ancient hospitality of an Archbishop of Canterbury'[6]. At Lambeth Palace, as at Corpus Christi College, he took great and detailed interest in the garden and, as was common in Tudor households, herbs and roots for the kitchen as well as flowers and fruit were grown there. He also had the gardens well stocked for the kitchen at his house at Bekesbourne in Kent, where he and his family spent as much time as they could.

Matthew's position as Archbishop brought another change to Margaret's life. She now had a greater part in ceremonial events. She appeared at the Archbishop's banquets and was referred to as 'Your Grace', although at the same time she must have been well aware of the difficulty of her position. She was, by all accounts, a good and frugal housewife who ran her household well, making Matthew's surroundings comfortable and relieving him of all domestic worries. During this time she met Bess of Hardwick, who was then known as one of the most ambitious women of the age. Although both women were running large households, they had markedly differing experiences of marriage. Margaret, by all accounts, was a devoted wife, protected by and supportive to her husband; while Bess was a strong, independent woman who buried many husbands, progressively increasing her wealth and social standing. It is not known how

---

6. Strype, Book 2, page 128.

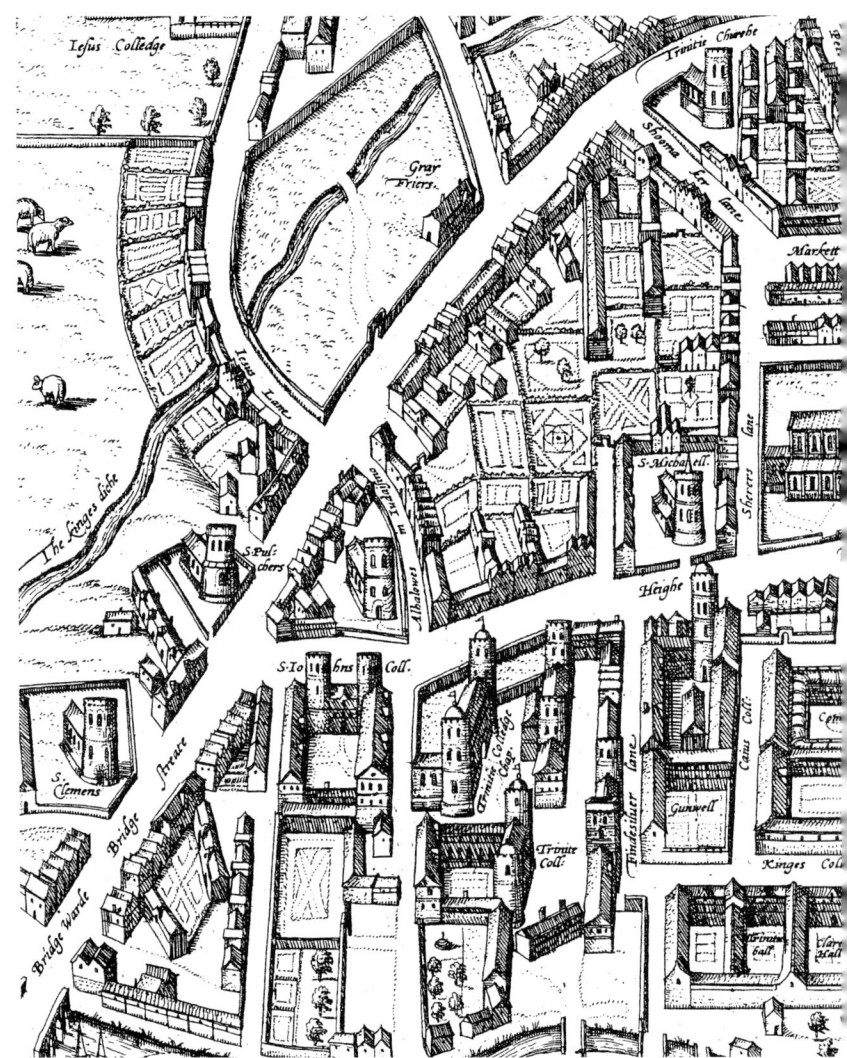

*Part of a plan of Cambridge showing Corpus Christi as Bene't College, from Braun and Hogen*

# A Proper Newe Booke of Cokerye

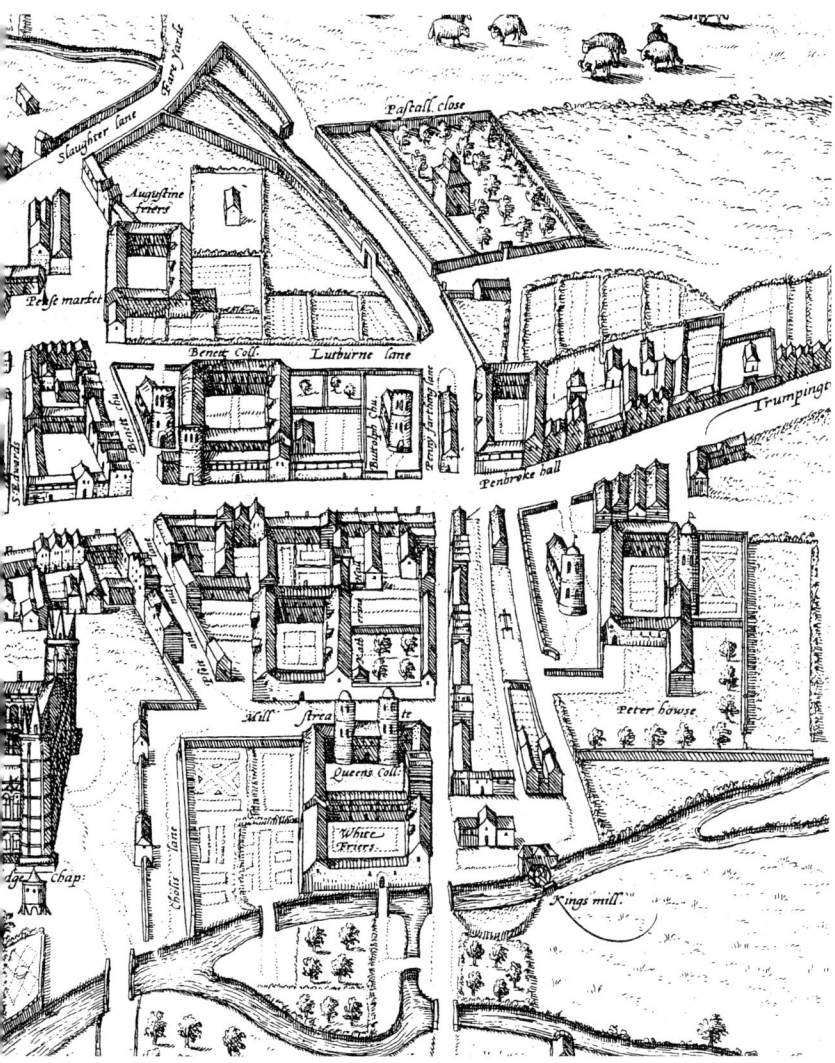

atus Orbis Terrarum 1573–1598.

she and Margaret met, but as Countess of Shrewsbury, Bess was for a time the virtual gaoler of Mary Queen of Scots, and like Margaret she was acquainted with Queen Elizabeth; they may well have met at Court. It is also known that Margaret gave Bess a copy of Matthew's metrical version of the Psalms.

These were days when there was elaborate protocol for ceremonial meals. Such occasions involved detailed planning and execution. The table was laid with much care and ceremony. Etiquette was observed in the seating order and in the placing of the salt which divided the more important guests from the rest. Food was always tasted in advance for fear of poison. Even the napkins were tested by a 'kiss of tentation'. This was considered a necessary precaution in the sixteenth century; Bess of Hardwick was personally affected by attempts to poison her. She and her third husband Sir William St Loe were both victims of an attempted poisoning by his brother Edward – he attempted murder to try to prevent the loss of his inheritance through Bess and William's marriage. In the play *The White Devil*, by John Webster, written early in the seventeenth century, the heroine is murdered by kissing a poisoned picture of her husband. It is not surprising that dining at ceremonial occasions in Tudor times was considered a hazardous business.

Cooks in the sixteenth century used a large variety of fresh produce, combined with spices such as ginger, cinnamon and rosewater brought back from abroad during the Crusades and introduced to cooking in England. Saffron from the fields of Essex was used. Sugar had long been in use by that time and was popular amongst the wealthy. New fruits and vegetables came from southern Europe and many dried fruits such as raisins, prunes and dates were imported. A great variety of fish, meat and birds was prepared in the kitchens of the wealthy. Fish was always served on Fridays in Lent; during Elizabeth's reign Wednesday was also declared a fish day, to encourage the fishing industry. The produce in the kitchen and on the table of a household was controlled by the season as well as by the depth of the householder's purse. For special feasts in a wealthy household, a large number of staff worked under the direction of supervisors who managed the different areas of preparation and cooking. The main meal was usually served close to midday, with a lighter supper in the early evening. Cooks in the sixteenth century were aware of many methods used today, such as separating eggs and using the yolks to thicken sauces and the beaten-up whites for desserts. *A Proper Newe Booke of Cokerye* contains several examples of these methods. The recipes describe copious use of spices with seasonal produce.

   The Parkers presided over many festive occasions and it is possible that *A Proper Newe Booke of Cokerye* was used when preparing the food for some of these events. One of the most significant was in 1560 when Queen Elizabeth, together with the Privy Council, came to Lambeth Palace to dine with the Archbishop.

   The Queen did not like any man to be married – let alone the clergy. She even tried to forbid married clergy from occupying deaneries, but was prevented by her new Archbishop. Matthew was naturally concerned for his own wife's welfare should he predecease her. Rules of inheritance were unclear, so Matthew had some of his estates placed in Margaret's ownership under her maiden name to ensure that there would be no difficulty when he died. He also arranged for her to inherit the house at

*Morton's Tower, built in 1490. (Lambeth Palace Library)*

Bekesbourne and the Duke of Norfolk's house in Lambeth, which he now owned. This was a wise precaution as the Duke of Norfolk had himself been beheaded for accidentally committing high treason. As it transpired, Matthew's caution was unnecessary as Margaret predeceased him by a number of years.

The Queen's visit to Lambeth was a significant one. The fact that she had agreed to dine there may well have led Margaret to believe that she had been accepted as 'Her Grace'. However, when Matthew presented his wife to the Queen, Elizabeth first gave Matthew very special thanks and then, turning to Margaret, was reputed to have said, 'And you, Madam I may not call you, and Mistress I am ashamed to call you, but yet I do thank you.' As a result of the Queen's unwillingness to accept Margaret's status wholeheartedly, wives of bishops in the Church of England remain to this day without the official status of ladyship when their husbands become members of the House of Lords. After Matthew Parker's death it was a long time before there was another married Archbishop of Canterbury.

Matthew Parker's term as Archbishop was momentous. It is recognised today that he occupies a prominent place in the history of England. He amended the Thirty-Nine Articles which govern the Anglican Church and which are still in use today. He was obliged to reconcile a group of clergy who held many different views and had come through difficult and changing times. The subject of vestments was fraught with difficulty, and fear of papal influence abounded. Clerical marriage was generally unpopular, and the relaxation of the rules meant that young priests often made unsuitable marriages. Laws had to be passed which required prospective wives of priests to be vetted very carefully.

A PROPER NEWE BOOKE OF COKERYE

Map of Westminster (Braun and Hogenberg). (Lambeth Palace Library)

A Proper Newe Booke of Cokerye

STILLIARDS) Hansa, Gothica dictio, conuentum, vel congregationem sonans, multarum ciuitatum est confoederata Societas, tum ob praefita Regibus, ac Ducib. beneficia: tum ob securam terra, mariq́ue, mercatura tractationem, tum denique, ad trāquillam Rerumpub. pacem, & ad modestam adolescentum institutionem conseruandam, instituta: plurimor̄ Regum, ac Principum, maximè Angliæ, Galliæ, Daniæ, ac Magnæ Moscouiæ, nec non Flandriæ, ac Brabantiæ Du cum priuilegijs, ac immunitatib. eornata fuit. Habet ea quatuor Emporia, Cuntores quidam vocant, in quibus ciuitatum negotiatores resident, suasq́ue mercatus Lerient. Hor. alterum hîc Londini. domestica oeconomia nitet, habens domum Gildehalla Teutonici, qua vulgo Stilhard, nuncupat.

There was huge controversy about the marriage of priests; a book on this subject was published anonymously in 1561. Matthew Parker worked his way through all these matters with much wisdom and due diligence, so that by the time he died the Anglican Church was established on a firm basis. Along with his many formal duties, unexpected events had also to be dealt with. In 1563 there was pestilence and famine in England, and he was obliged to declare a special fast. All people between the ages of 16 and 60, with some exceptions, were to eat only one meal on Wednesdays. It was to be simple and without large amounts of meat or fish. This was combined with extra prayers and general caution about food wastage.

As Archbishop, Matthew entertained in style at Canterbury as well as at Lambeth. In 1565 he gave three feasts. The first was at Whitsun and lasted for three days, beginning with a service in the Cathedral. The Archbishop sat at the top table and on his left were seated the important male guests in order of rank, the women sat likewise on his right. At the feast there would have been more than one sitting so that a large number of people could be invited. The second feast was held on Trinity Sunday with similar timings and ceremonies. The third and grandest feast was held during the Assizes, when the judges on the circuit were invited to dine, together with their staff and associates – who would have included trumpeters, jesters and javelin-men. The hall would have been richly decorated and food and drink served by the Archbishop's servants. Again there would have been several sittings until everyone had eaten their fill. This last feast allowed only gentlemen in the hall. Their wives would have been entertained by Margaret in the inner chambers. However, women were generally included as much as possible in the Archbishop's entertaining because of Matthew's strong belief in matrimony and his appreciation of the support given to him by his wife.

The Parkers' sons both married the daughters of bishops. In 1566 the eldest son had a daughter who was called Margaret after her grandmother. Later this son had a son named Matthew after his grandfather, and there were five other children. The younger son married in 1570. One might speculate that *A Proper Newe Booke of Cokerye* was much in use for family meals as well as for ceremonial occasions during the later years of Margaret and Matthew's lives.

The Parkers continued to divide their time between Lambeth and Canterbury. In 1570 they returned as usual to Lambeth from Canterbury, travelling first by coach and then by river. Although there was now concern about the Archbishop's health, it was Margaret who developed a fever, soon after their return. She died on 17 August in that year. She was only 51 when she died. Matthew recorded her end in his diary. 'This Margaret, my most dearly beloved and virtuous wife, who lived with me some twenty-six years, and died right Christianly on the 17th of August, 1570, about eleven o'clock in the forenoon, and lies buried in the Duke of Norfolk's chapel at Lambeth.' Matthew died in 1575, five years after Margaret, and he must have missed her love and support deeply during his last years.. He died at the then advanced age of 72. According to tradition 72 poor men attended his funeral.

Matthew and Margaret Parker lived in the Master's Lodge at Corpus Christi College nearly five centuries ago. The tradition of the Master and his family living in the Master's Lodge continues to the present day.

Many dramatic events have affected the College over the centuries. In 1630 the plague came to Cambridge, and the Master at that time, Henry Butts, committed suicide in despair after trying to help control the epidemic. His ghost is said to haunt the College in the vicinity of the old Master's Lodge. Richard Love became Master during the Civil War; he saved the College silver by distributing it among the Fellows and then sending them on leave of absence. The silver, including the pieces left to the College by Matthew Parker, was returned after the war and is still in use today; placed prominently on the tables on feast days. The New Court, including the current Master's Lodge, was built early in the nineteenth century and the Master at that time, John Lamb, moved there with his wife and brought up a family of fourteen children. Entertaining and hospitality have also evolved in the Master's Lodge. During the Mastership of Robert Townley Caldwell, in the early years of the twentieth century, many more Members of the College, particularly undergraduates, began to be invited into the Lodge. This set the pattern of entertaining for a succession of Masters and their wives who have continued the tradition of hospitality in the College to the present day.

Since the publication of *A Proper Newe Booke of Cokerye* numerous cookery books have been written and cooking methods have evolved. Nevertheless this little volume occupies a unique position in the history of cookery in this country.

# Facsimile of A Proper Newe Booke of Cokerye

## With Interpretation

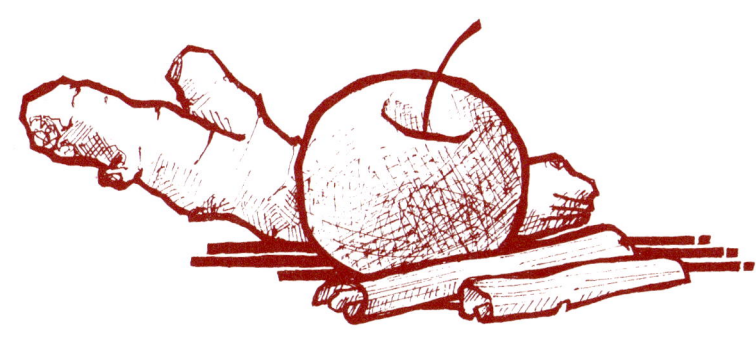

# ¶ A Proper

newe Booke of Cokerye,
declarynge what maner of
meates be beste in season,
for al times in the yere,
and how they ought
to be dressed, and
serued at the ta
ble, bothe for
flesshe dayes,
and fysshe
dayes.
With a newe addition, verye ne-
cessarye for all them that
delyghteth in Co-
kerye.
(⸪)

# A Proper Newe Booke of Cokerye

Declaring what manner of
meats be best in season,
for all times of the year,
and how they ought
to be dressed, and
served at the table,
both for flesh
days and fish
days.
With a new addition, very
necessary for all those
who delight in
cookery.

¶ The booke of Cokerye.

**B**Rawne is beste from a fortenyghte before Mychalemas tyll lente. Beefe and Bacon is good all tymes in the yere. Mutton is good at all tymes, but from Easter to mydsommer it is worste. A fatte pygge is euer in season. A goose is worste in Midsommer mone, and beste in stubble tyme, but when they be yong grene geese, then they be beste. Veale is beste in Januarye, and February, and all other tymes good. Lambe and yonge kydde is beste betwene Christmas and lente, and good from Easter to Witsontyde. Kyd is euer good, Hennes be good at all tymes, but beste from Nouember to lente, Fat Capons be euer in season. Pecockes be euer good, but whē they be yong and of a good stature, they be as good as fesantes, and so be yonge grouces. Ginettes be beste betwene all Hallowen dayes and Lente. A Mallarde is good after a froste, tyll candelmas, so is a Teile and other wilde foule that swymmeth. A wodcocke is beste from Octobre to Lente: and so be all other byrdes as Ousels, and Thrusselles, Robins

A.ij.

# The Booke of Cokerye

Brawn (usually wild boar meat) is best from a fortnight before Michaelmas (about mid September) until Lent (between February and March). Beef and bacon are good all year round. Mutton is always good but is not as good to eat between Easter (forty days after the beginning of Lent) and mid summer. A fat pig is always in season. A goose is worst in the midsummer month (June) and best in stubble time (autumn).

Geese are best eaten when young.

Veal is good at any time but best in January and February. Lamb and young kid (goat) are best between Christmas and Lent, and good from Easter to Whitsun (April to June). Goat is always good. Hens are good at all times, but are best from November to Lent. Fat capons are always in season. (Capons are young male chickens which have been castrated – between six and ten months old, and fattened for the table.)

Peacocks are always good and when young and of a good size are as good as pheasants, as are young grouse.

Cygnets are best between All Hallows Day (1 November) and Lent. A mallard is good after a frost and until Candelmas (early February), so is a teal and other wild fowl that swim. A woodcock is best from October until Lent, and so are other birds such as blackbirds and thrushes, robins and others.

## The booke

bins, and suche other. Herons, Curlus, Craue, Bitture, Bustarde be at all times good, but beste in wynter. Fesauntes, Partriche, and Rayle, be euer good but beste when they be taken with a hauke. Quayle and Larkes bee euer in seaſon. Connyes be euer good and ſo is a doo. A hare is euer good, but beſte from October to Lente. A gelded dere whether he be falowe or readde, is euer in seaſon. A Pollarde is ſpeciall good in maye, at Midſommer he is a Bucke, and is verye good tyll holye Rood daye before Mighelmas, ſo lykewyſe is a ſtagge, but he is principal in Maye. A barren doo is beſte in wynter. A Pricked and a ſorell ſyſter, is euer in ſeaſon. Chekins be euer good, and ſo bee Pigions yf they be younge

¶ Here after foloweth the order of meates, howe they muſte be ſerued at the Table, with their ſauces for fleſhe dayes at dynner.

¶ The fyrſte courſe.

Potage

Herons, curlews, crane, bittern and bustard are good at all times, but best in the winter. Pheasants, partridges and landrail are always good, but best when taken with a hawk. Quail and larks are always in season.

Connies (rabbits more than a year old) are always good, and so is a doe (a female rabbit). A hare is always good but best from October to Lent.

A gelded (castrated) deer, whether he is a fallow deer or a red deer, is always in season. A pollard (a stag without horns) is especially good in May. At midsummer a buck (male fallow deer) is best until Michaelmas, and up until Holyrood Day (14 September); as is a stag (male red deer). A barren doe (female fallow deer) is best in winter. A buck in his second year and a hind (a female red deer, three years old) are always in season.

Chickens are always good and so are pigeons if they are young.

Here follows the order of meats, and how they must be served at table with their sauces for meat days at dinner.

¶ Potage or stewed broath,
Bolde meate or stewed meate
Chekins and Bacon
Powdred beyfe
Pyes
Goose
Pygge
Roosted beyfe
Roosted veale
Custarde.
　　¶ The seconde course.
Roosted Lambe
Roosted Capons
Roosted Connies
Chekins
Pehennes
Baken Veneson
Tarte.

　　¶ The fyrst seruice at supper.
　¶ Potage or sewe
A sallette
A pygges petytoe
Powdred beyfe slyced
A Shoulder of Mutton or a Brest
Veale
Lambe
Custarde.

A.iii.　　The

## The Fyrste Course

Potage (vegetable soup) or stewed broth (soup with meat)
Boiled or stewed meat
Chickens and bacon
Salted beef
Pies
Goose
Pig
Roast beef
Roast veal
Custard (made with a piecrust, or a batter like Yorkshire pudding)

## The Seconde Course

Roast lamb
Roast capons
Roast connies
Chickens
Peahens
Baked venison
Tart

## The Fyrste Service at Supper

Potage or sewe (soup with meat in it)
Salad (this could be fish with onions etc.)
A pig's pettytoe (could be trotters or chitterlings, or made with goose giblets)
Sliced salted beef
Shoulder or breast of mutton
Veal
Lamb
Custard

The Booke.

### ❧ The seconde course.

Capons roosted
Connies roosted
Chekins roosted
Pigeons roosted
Larckes roosted
A pye of pygeons or Chekins
Baken venison.
Tarte

### ❧ The seruyce at dyner.

Brawne and mustarde
Capons stewed or in whyte broath
A pestle of venesou vpon a browes.
A chyne of beyfe, and a brest of mutton boylde.
Chuettes of pyes of fyne mutton
Thre grene gese in a dyshe, sorel sauce, for a stubble gose, mustarde, and vineger.
After all halowen daye, a swan.
Sauce chadel.
A pygge.
A dubble rybbe of beyf roosted, sauce, pepper and vyneger.
A loyne of veale or a brest     Sauce
Halfe a lambe or a kyd     orengers
Two capons roosted,     Sauce wyne and salte, ale and salt, except it be vppon soppes.

Two

## The Seconde Coorse

Roast capons
Roast connies
Roast chickens
Roast pigeons
Roast larks
Chicken or pigeon pie
Baked venison
Tart

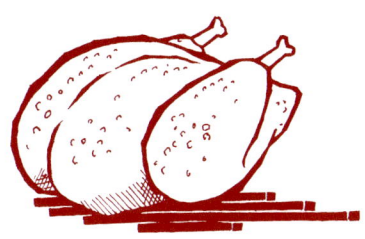

## The Service at Dyner

Brawn (lean boar meat) and mustard

Capons, stewed or in white broth

A pestel (leg) of venison on a browes (in broth)

Shin of beef and breast of mutton, boiled

Small pies of fine mutton

Three green geese in a dish (young geese up until six months old) in sorrel sauce; for a stubble goose (wild goose) a sauce with mustard and vinegar

After All Hallows Day, a swan with a chadel sauce (this could be made with chopped liver and entrails, boiled with blood, bread, wine, vinegar, pepper, cloves and ginger)

A pig

A double rib of roast beef with vinegar and pepper sauce

A loin or breast of veal } with orange sauce
Half a lamb or goat

Two roast capons with wine sauce and salt

Ale and salt to season, except with soppes (small pieces of bread – sometimes toasted)

Of Cokerye.
Two pasties of falow dere in a dyshe.
A custarde
A dyshe of Leches.

### ❡ The seconde course.

Jellye.
Peacocke    Sauce, wyne, and salte.
Two connies or halfe a dosyn rabets.
Sauce mustarde and suger.
Halfe a dosyn chekyns vpon sorell soppes.
Halfe a dosyn pigeons
Mallarde
Teyle        ( Sauce, mustarde
Bulles       ( and verges.
Storke
Heronshewe
Crane        (
Curlew       )( Sauce galentyne.
Bitture      (
Bustarde
Fesande    Sauce water and salt with onyons slyced.
Halfe a dosen woodcockes
Sauce mustarde and suger.
Halfe a dosen partriches
Halfe a dosen tayles.
Sauced as the fesants.

A.iiii.

Two pasties of fallow deer in a dish
A custard
A dish of leches (usually made with milk, flour, sugar and lemon)

## The Seconde Course

Jelly
Peacock with salt and wine sauce
Two connies or half a dozen rabbits
Mustard and sugar sauce
Half a dozen chickens on sorrel soppes
Half a dozen pigeons

Mallard
Teal
Gulls — with mustard and verges sauce (verges is a green sauce, sometimes the by-product of wine making and sometimes made from crab apples)
Stork
Heron

Crane
Curlew — with sauce galantine (this could be made with brown bread and vinegar)
Bittern
Bustard

Pheasant with sauce made with water and sliced onions
Half a dozen woodcocks with mustard and sugar
Half a dozen partridges
Half a dozen teal
Sauce as for pheasants

The booke
A dosen of Quayles
A dyshe of Larkes
Two pasties of redde deare in a dyshe.
Tarte
Genfbread
Fritteris.

¶ Seruice for fyshe dayes.
Butter
A sallet with harde Egges.
Potage of Sande Eles and Lamperns
Reade hearynge, grene broyled strawed vpon.
whyte herynge (
Lynge       ( Mustarde.
Haburdyn. (
Salte Samon minced
Sauce, Mustarde and Vergis and a lyttle Suger.
Powdred Conger (
Shadde       ( Sauce, vineger.
Makrell. (
Whytinge   Sauce, wyth the lyuer and mustarde.
Plyace,   Sauce, forel, or wyne and salte or mustarde or vergys.
Thornebacke Sauce, lyuer and mustard, peper, and salte strawed vpon after it is brused.
Freshe codde.   Sauce, grene sauce.
Base.

A dozen quail
A dish of larks
Two pasties of red deer in a dish
Tart
Gingerbread
Fritters

## Service for Fyshe Dayes

Butter
Salad with hard-boiled eggs
Broth of sand eels and river lampreys
Smoked herring with fried parsley

Fresh herring
Ling } with mustard
Haburde (spotted cod)

Minced salted salmon, with mustard and verges sauce with a little sugar

Salted conger
(sea fish of the eel family)
Shad } with sauce with liver and mustard
Mackerel
Whiting

Plaice with sorrel sauce, or sauce made with wine and salt or mustard or verges sauce

Thornback with liver and mustard sauce, with pepper and salt sprinkled on it after bruising

Fresh cod with green sauce (made with fresh green herbs such as parsley and mint with vinegar)

of Cokerye.

Base
Mullette
Eles vpon soppes
Roche vpon soppes
Perche
Pyke in pyke sauce.
Troute vpon soppes
Tenche in gelly or in gressell
Custarde.

### The seconde course

Flownders or floer in pyke sauce
Freshe Salmon
Freshe Conger
Brette ( Sauce, vineger.
Turbutte
Holybutte.
Breme vpon soppes
Carpe vpon soppes
Soles or any other fyshes fryed
Roosted Eles  Sauce, the dryp=
Roosted Lamperns  pynge.
Roosted purpos  Sauce, galentine
Freshe Sturgeon
Creues (
Crabbe ( Sauce, vineger.
Shrimpes (
Baken Lamprey.
                    Tarte

Bass
Mullet
Eels on soppes
Roach on soppes
Perch
Pike in pike sauce
Trout on soppes
Tench in jelly or soup
Custard

## The Seconde Course

Flounders or floex (kind of flounder) in pike sauce
Fresh salmon
Fresh conger

Brette (a kind of turbot)
Turbot } with vinegar sauce
Holybutte (halibut)

Bream on soppes
Carp on soppes
Sole or any other fried fish

Roast eels
Roast lampreys } with dripping sauce

Roast porpoise
Fresh sturgeon } with sauce galantine

Crayfish
Crab
Shrimps } with vinegar sauce
Baked lamprey

### The Booke

| | |
|---|---|
| Tarte | Chese |
| Fygees | Raysyns |
| Apples | Peares |
| Almondes blanched. | |

#### ¶ To dresse a crabe.

Fyrste take awaye all the legges, and the heades, and then take all the fysh out of the shelle, and make the shell as cleane as ye canne, and putte the meate into a dysshe, and butter it vppon a chafyng-dysshe of coles, and putte therto synamon and suger and a lytle vyneger, and when ye haue chafed it and seasoned it, then putte the meate in the shelle agayne, and bruse the heades, and set them vpon the dysshe syde and serue it.

#### ¶ To make a stewed broath for Capons, mutton, beyfe or any other hoate meate, and also a broathe for al maner of freshe fyshe.

Take halfe a handefull of rosemary, and as muche of tyme, and bynde it on a bundel wyth threde after it is wasshen, and put it in the potte, after that the potte is cleane skummed, and lette it boyle a whyle, then cutte soppes of white breade, and put them in a great charger, and

| | |
|---|---|
| Tart | Cheese |
| Figs | Raisins |
| Apples | Pears |
| Blanched almonds | |

### To Dresse a Crabe

First take away the legs and heads. (These could be the claws, but it is possible that a lobster is meant here.) Take the fish out of the shell, and make the shell as clean as you can, and put the meat in a dish and add butter. Put in a buttered dish over a chafing dish (a vessel filled with charcoal) to heat. Add cinnamon, sugar and a little vinegar. When you have warmed and seasoned it, put the meat back into the shell. Break up the heads and set them beside the dish and serve.

### To Make a Stewed Broath for Capons, Mutton, Beyfe or any other Hoate Meate, and also a Broathe for al maner of Freshe Fyshe

Take a handful of rosemary and the same amount of thyme. Wash this and bind into a bundle with thread. Put it into the cleaned pot (with water) and after skimming off the scum let it boil for a while. (This probably means that the meat was already cooked and removed, the pot cleaned and the stock made before putting the meat back.)

## Of cokerye.

and put it on the same skaldyngebroath, and when it is soken ynoughe, strayne it throughe a strayner wyth a quantity of wyne or good ale, so that it be not tarte, and when it is strayned, powre it in a pot and than putte in youre raysons and prunes, and so lette them boyle tyll the meate be ynoughe. Yf the broathe be to swete, putte in the more wyne, or els a lyttle vyneger.

### ℭ To make Pyes.

Pyes of mutton or beif must be fyne mynced and ceasoned wyth pepper and salte, and a lyttle saffron to coloure it, suet or marrow a good quantite, a lyttle vyneger, prunes, greate raysins, and dates, take the fatte{s}t of the broathe of powdred beyfe, and yf you wyll haue paeste royall, take butter and yolkes of egges, and to tempre the flowre to make the paeste.

### ℭ To bake Uenefon.

Take nothynge but pepper and salte, but lette it haue ynoughe, and yf the Uenefon be leane, larde it throughe wyth bacon.

### ℭ To roofte Uenefon.

Roofted Uenefon muste haue vyneger

Then cut up soppes of white bread and put them in a large dish and pour the hot broth over them. When it is soaked enough, strain through a strainer with a quantity of wine or good ale, so that the taste is not too tart. After straining, put it into a pot, add raisins and prunes, and let the meat boil until tender. If the broth is too sweet, put in more wine or a little vinegar.

### To Make Pyes

The mutton or beef must be minced finely for pies and seasoned with salt and pepper, and a little saffron to colour it. Also add a good quantity of suet or marrow, a little vinegar, prunes, large raisins and dates. Take the best of the broth, and if you would like a paste royal, take butter and egg yolks and mix this broth with some flour to make the pastry (paste royal is likely to have been pieces of pastry for garnish).

### To Bake Veneson

Take nothing but pepper and salt, but season it well, and if the venison is lean, lard it with bacon.

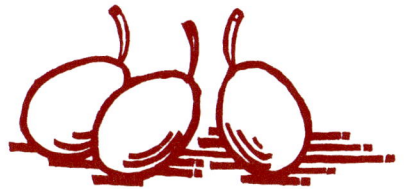

#### The booke

ger, Suger, and Cinomome, and butter boylded vpon a chafingdyshe with cooles, but the sauce maye not bee to tarte, and then laye the Veneson vpon the sauce.

¶ Chekins vpon soppes.

Take sorel sauce a good quantite, and put in Cinomome and Suger, and let it boyle, and powre it vpon the soppes, and then laye on the chekins.

¶ A Pyke sauce for a Pyke, Breme, Perche, Roche, Carpe, Eles, Floykes, and al maner of brouke fyshe.

Take a posye of Rosemary and time, and bynde them together, and put in also a quantitye of perselye not bounde, and put into the caudron of water, salte and yeste, and the herbes, and lette them boyle a pretye whyle, then putte in the fysshe, and a good quantitye of butter, and let them boyle a good season, and you shall haue good Pyke sauce.

For all these fysshes aboue wrytten, yf they muste bee broyled, take sauce for them, butter, peepper, and vyneger, and boyle it vpon a chafyngdyshe, and then laye the broyled fyshe vppon the dyshe, but for Eeles and freshe Salmon nothing but

### To Rooste Veneson

Roast venison must have a sauce of vinegar, sugar, cinnamon and butter, boiled in a chafing dish and set on charcoal. The sauce must not be too tart. Then lay the venison in the sauce.

### Chekins Upon Soppes

Take a good quantity of sorrel sauce, add cinnamon and sugar, and let it boil. Pour it on the soppes and lay the chickens on top.

### A Pyke Sauce for a Pyke, Breme, Perche, Roche, Carpe, Eles, Floykes, and al maner of Brouke Fyshe

Take a posy of rosemary and thyme and bind them together, add a quantity of unbound parsley and put it in a large pot of water. Add salt and yeast to the herbs and boil for a good period of time. Then put in the fish with a good quantity of butter and bring back to the boil, and you should have a good pike sauce.

For all those fish named above, if they are broiled (cooked dry over hot coals), make this sauce for them. Take butter, pepper and vinegar and heat in a dish over charcoal and then lay the broiled fish on the dish. For eels and fresh salmon use nothing but a sauce of pepper and vinegar which is over boiled (boiled so as to overflow the pot). If you fry them you must take a good quantity of parsley and, after the fish is fried, put the parsley into the frying pan and let it fry in the butter. Then put it on the fried fish. Fry plaice, whiting and other similar fish like this, except for eels, fresh salmon and conger, which should never be fried but baked, boiled, roasted or sodden (boiled).

of Cokerye.

but Pepper and vyneger ouer boyled. And also yf you wyll frye them, you muste take a good quantitie of persely, after the fyshe is fryed, put in the persely into the fryinge panne, and let it frye in the butter, and take it vp and put it on the fryed fyshe, and frye plaice, whyttinge and suche other fyshe, excepte Eles, freshe Salmon, Conger, whiche be neuer fryed but baken, boyled, roosted, or sodden.

### ¶ To make a Custarde.

A Custarde the cofyn muste be fyrste hardened in the ouen, and then take a quart of creame and fyue or syxe yolkes of egges, and beate them well together, and put them into the creame, and put in Suger and small Reysyns and Dates sliced, and put into the cofyn butter or els marowe, but on the fyshe dates put in butter.

¶ Here after foloweth a newe
Booke of Cokerye.

### ¶ To make cleare Iellye.

¶ Take two calues feete and a shoulder of Veale, and sette it vpon the fyre in a fayre potte wyth a gallon of water and

### To Make a Custarde

The coffin or crust for the custard must be first hardened in the oven (baked blind). Then take a quart of cream and beat up five or six egg yolks, and add them to the cream. Then add sugar and small raisins and sliced dates, and put the mixture into the pastry dish and add butter or marrow, but on fish days just add butter.

### Hereafter Followeth a Newe Booke of Cokerye

### To Make Cleare Jellye

Take two calves' feet and a shoulder of veal and put on the fire in a clean pot with a gallon of water and a gallon of claret wine. Then let it boil until it becomes jelly, and then strain and add cinnamon, ginger and sugar and a little turnsole (blue colouring from lichen) to colour it to your discretion.

### The Booke

and a gallon of claret wyne, than lette it boyle tyll it be Iellye, and than take it vp and strayne it, and putte thereto Synamon, Gynger, and Suger, and a lyttle turnesole to coloure it after youre dyscrecion.

### To make a dysshe full of Snowe.

Take a pottell of swete thycke creame, and the whytes of eyghte egges, and beate them altogether wyth a spone, then putte them in youre creame and a saucer full of Rose water, and a dyshe full of Suger wyth all, then take a stycke and make it cleane, and than cutte it in the ende foure square, and therwith beate all the aforesayde thynges together, and euer as it ryseth take it of and put it into a Collaunder, this done, take one apple and set it in the myddes of it, and a thicke busshe of Rosemary, and set it in the myddes of the platter, then caste your Snowe vppon the Rosemarye, and fyll your platter therwith. And yf you haue wafers caste some in wyth all and thus serue them forthe.

### To frye Beanes.

Take youre Beanes and boyle them, and

## To Make a Dyshefull of Snowe

Take a pottell (two quarts) of thick sweet cream and beat the whites of eight eggs together with a spoon. Then add the cream with a saucer full of rosewater and a dishful (cupful) of sugar. Take a clean stick and square the end, and beat all the ingredients together, and when it has risen take it out and put it into a colander. This done, take one apple and set it in the middle of it. Place a thick piece of rosemary in the middle of a plate and pile the mixture on top of it. If you have some wafers add these and serve.

of Cokerye.

and putte them into a frynge panne with a dysshe of butter, and one or two onions, and so lette them frye tyll they be browne al together, than caste a lyttle salte vpon them, and than serue them forthe.

### To make Panne puffe.

Take the stuffe of Stocke frytters, and for hys paest take a quantite of ale, and a lytle yest and Suger, Mace, and Saffron, than heate it on a chafyndysshe, and put it to youre floure with the yolcke of a rawe egge, and so after this maner make vp youre paest.

### To make Blewe manger.

Take a capon and cut out the brawne of hym a lyue and perboyle the brawne tyll the flesshe come from the bone, and then drye hym as drye as you canne, in a fayre clothe, then take a payre of cardes, and carde hym as small as is possyble, and than take a pottell of mylke and a pottel of creame, and halfe a pounde of Rye flower, and pour carded brawne of the capon, and putte all into a pan, and stere it al together and set it vpon the fyre, and wha it begyn-

### To Frye Beanes

Take the beans (probably broad beans) and boil them, and then put into a frying pan with a dishful of butter, and one or two onions, and let them fry until browned, then add a little salt and serve.

### To Make Panne Puffe

(Stock fritters were like dumplings, containing marrow, fruit and a variety of spices.)

Take the mixture of stock fritters and for the paste take a quantity of ale and a little yeast and sugar, mace and saffron. Then heat it in a dish over charcoal and add flour with the yolk of a raw egg and in this way make the paste.

### To Make a Blewe Manger

(This was usually made from white meat, generally capon with flour, sugar and cream.)

Take a capon and cut out the brawn (lean meat) and liver and parboil the brawn until the flesh comes away from the bone. Then dry it as much as possible in a clean cloth. Cut the capon up in small pieces with a wire card or comb, and then take a pottell of milk and a pottell of cream and half a pound of rye flour. Cut up the brawn of the capon and put it all in a pan, and stir it all and put it over the fire. When it begins to boil, put in half a pound of sugar and a saucerful of rosewater and let it boil until it is very thick. Then put it aside to cool in a dish and slice it and serve.

### The Booke

begynneth to boyle put thereto halfe a pounde of beaten Suger and a sauserfull of Rose water, and so let it boyle tyll it be very thicke, then put it into a charger tyll it be colde, and then ye maye slyce it as ye doe lieche and so serue it in.

### ¶ To make Pyes of grene apples.

Take your apples and pare them cleane and core them as ye wyll a Quince, then make youre coffyn after this maner, take a lyttle fayre water and halfe a dyshe of butter and a lyttle Saffron, and sette all this vpon a chafyngdyshe tyll it be hoate, then temper your flower with this sayd licour, and the whyte of two egges, and also make your coffyn, and ceason your apples with Sinemone, Gynger and Suger ynoughe. Then putte them into your coffin and laye halfe a dyshe of butter aboue the, and so close your coffin, and so bake them.

### ¶ To bake chekins in lyke paest.

Take youre chekins and ceason them with a lytle Ginger & salte, and so putte them into youre cofin, and so put in them barberies

## To Make Pyes of Grene Apples

Take the apples and pare, clean and core them as you would a quince. Then make the coffin (pastry case) in this way. Take a little fresh water and half a dish (cup) of butter and a little saffron, and set it over heat until it warms up. Then add flour to this liquid and the white of two eggs and thus make the coffin. Season the apples with cinnamon, ginger and sugar to taste. Then put the mixture into the pastry case with some butter over it, and close and bake.

barberies, grapes, or goose beryes, and halfe a dyshe of butter, so cloose them vp, and sette them in the ouen, and when they are baken, take the yolkes of fyre egges, and a dyshfull of vergis and drawe them through a streyner and sette it vpon a chafingdyshe, then drawe youre baken chekins and put therto this foresayde egges and vergys, and thus serue them hoate.

### To bake pygeons in short paeste as you make to youre baken apples.

⁋Season youre pigeons with peper, saffron, cloues and mace, with vergis and salte, then putte them into youre paeste, and so cloose them vp, and bake them, they wyl bake in halfe an houre, then take them forthe, and yf ye thinke theym drye, take a lyttle vergis and butter and put in theim and so serue theym.

### To make vautes.

⁋Take the kydney of veale and per boyle it tyll it be tender, then take and choppe it small wyth the yolkes of three or foure egges, then season it wyth dates small cutte, small Reysons, Gynger

B.i.

## To Bake Chekins in Lyke Paest

Season the chickens with a little ginger and salt. Put them into the coffin (pastry case) and add barberries, grapes or gooseberries and half a dish (cup) of butter. Close up the pastry case and put into the oven. When baked, take the yolk of six eggs and a dishful of verges and strain and heat. Pour over the chickens and serve hot.

## To Bake Pygeons in Short Paeste as You Make to Youre Baken Apples

Season the pigeons with pepper, saffron, cloves and mace, and with verges and salt. Then put them in the pastry, and close them up and bake well for half an hour. Then take them out. If you think that they are too dry, add butter and more verges and then serve.

The boke

ger, suger, synamon, saffron, and a lyttle salte, and for the paest to laye it in, take a dosen of egges, bothe the whyte and the yolkes, and beate theym well al together, then take butter, and put it into a frying panne, and frye them as thynne as a pancake, then laye your stuffe therein, and so frye them together in a panne, and caste suger and gynger vpon it, and so serue it forthe.

¶ To make pescoddes.

Take mary bones and pull the mary hole out of them, and cutte it in two partes, then season it with suger, synamon, ginger, and a lytle salte, and make youre paeste as fyne as ye canne, and as shorte and thyn as ye canne, then frye theym in swete suette and caste vpon them a lyttle synamon and ginger, and so serue them at the table.

To make stocke frytures.

Take the same stuffe that you take to a baute, and that same paeste ye take for pescoddes, and ye maye frye them or els bake them.

To stewe Trypes.

Take a pynte of claret wyne, and set it

### To Make Vautes

(Vautes are a kind of fritter.)

Take kidney of veal and parboil until tender. Then chop it up small with the yolks of three or four eggs (usually hard boiled) and season with finely chopped dates, small raisins, ginger, sugar, cinnamon, saffron and a little salt. For the pastry to lay it on, take a dozen eggs, both whites and yolks, and beat them all together. Then take butter and put the beaten eggs in a frying pan and fry them as thin as a pancake. Then lay the mixture on this and continue to fry. Sprinkle with sugar and ginger and serve.

### To Make Pescoddes

(These would be the shape of peapods and similar to vautes and panne puffe.)

Take marrow bones and pull the marrow out whole. Cut it into two and season with sugar, cinnamon, ginger and a little salt. Make the pastry as fine as you can, and roll it out as thin as possible. Wrap it round the marrow mixture and fry the pieces in sweet suet. Sprinkle a little cinnamon and ginger on them and serve at the table.

### To Make Stock Frytures

Make the mixture as for the vautes and the same pastry as for the pescoddes, and fry or bake.

of Cokerye.

it vpon the fyre, and cutte youre trypes in small peces, and therto putte in a good quantitye of synamon and gynger, and also a slyced onyō or twayne, and so let them boyle halfe an houre, and then serue them vpon soppes,

### To make a pye of alowes.

Take a legge of mutton and cutte it in thyn slyces, and for stuffing of the same take persely, tyme and sauerye, and chop them smal, then temper among them thre or iiii. yolckes of harde egges chopt smal, and small reysons, dates cutte with mace, and a lyttle salte, then laye all these in the stekes, and then role them togeather. This done make youre pye, and laye all these therein, then ceason theym wyth a lyttle suger and synamon, saffron & salte, then cast vpon theym the yolckes of three or foure harde egges, and cut dates, wyth small raysynges, so close youre pye, and bake hym. Then for a syrope for it, take toosted breade, and a lyrtle claret wyne, and strayne them thyn togeather, and put thereto a lytle suger, synamon, and gynger, and putte it into youre pye, and then serue it forthe.

B.ii.

### To Stewe Trypes

Take a pint of claret wine, set it on the heat, and cut the tripe into small pieces. Put in a good quantity of cinnamon and ginger and also a sliced onion or two, and let it boil for half an hour and serve on soppes.

### To Make a Pye of Alowes
(These are like beef olives.)

Take a leg of mutton and cut into thin slices. For the stuffing take parsley, thyme and savory and chop up small. Then add three or four yolks of hard-boiled eggs chopped up finely with small raisins, dates cut up with mace, and a little salt. Lay this mixture on the mutton slices and roll them up.

This done, make the pie. Lay all these slices in the pie dish, then season them with a little sugar and cinnamon, saffron and salt. Lay on them the yolks of three or four hard-boiled eggs and chopped dates, with small raisins, and close up the pie and bake. Then for a syrup (sauce) take toasted bread and a little claret wine and strain them together. Add a little sugar, cinnamon and ginger and put into the pie and serve.

(Before going to the table the syrup would be poured in through the hole left for the steam.)

## The Booke

### To make 3out paest for tarte.

Take fyne floure and a cutfey of fayre water and a dyfshe of swete butter and a lyttel saffron, and the yolckes of two egges and make it thynne and as tender as ye maye.

### To make a tarte of beanes.

Take beanes and boyle them tender in fayre water, then take theym oute and breake them in a morter and strayne them with the yolckes of foure egges, curde made of mylke, then ceason it vp with suger and halfe a dyfshe of butter and a lytle synamon and bake it.

### To make a tarte of goseberies.

Take goseberies and parboyle them in whyte wyne, claret or ale, and boyle with all a lyttle whyte breade, then take them vp, and drawe them throughe a strayner as thycke as you can with the yolckes of syxe egges, then seafon it vp with suger, halfe a dyfshe of butter, so bake it.

### To make a tarte of medlers.

Take medlers when they be rotten, and bray them with the yolckes of foure egges, then ceason it vp wyth suger and sinamon and swete butter, and so bake it.

To

### To Make Short Paest for Tarte
(Pastry)

Take fine flour and a little fresh water and a dish of sweet butter and a little saffron, and the yolks of two eggs. Make it as thin and tender as you can.

### To Make a Tarte of Beanes

Take the beans and boil them until tender in fresh water. Then take them out and crush them in a mortar and strain with the yolks of four eggs, and curd made of milk. Then season with sugar and half a dish (cup) of butter and a little cinnamon and bake.

### To Make a Tarte of Goseberies

Take gooseberries and parboil them in white wine, claret or ale, and then boil with a little white bread. Then take them out and strain through a strainer with the yolks of six eggs. Season with sugar, half a dish (cup) of butter and bake.

### To Make a Tarte of Medlers

(Medlars are still grown today; they are like small apples)

Pick the medlars when they are overripe, and beat them with the yolks of four eggs, then season with sugar, cinnamon and sweet butter, and bake.

#### Of Cokerye.

##### To make a tarte of damsons.

Take damsons and boyle theym in wyne, eyther red or claret, and put there to a dosen of peares, or els whyte bread too make theym styffe wyth all, then drawe theym vp wyth the yolkes of fyve egges and swete butter & so bake it.

##### To make a tarte of borage floures.

Take borage floures and perboyle them tender, then strayne them wyth the yolkes of three or foure egges, and swete curdes, or els take three or foure apples, and perboyle wythal and strayne them with swete butter and a lyttle mace and so bake it.

##### To make a tarte of marigoldes, prymroses, or cousslips.

Take the same stuffe to euery of them that you do to the tarte of borage, and the same ceasonynge.

##### To make a tarte of strawberyes.

Take and strayne theym wyth the yolkes of foure egges, and a lyttle whyte breade grated, then season it vp wyth suger and swete butter and so bake it.

##### To make a tarte of Cheryes.

Take all thinges that ye do the tarte

B.iii. of

### To Make a Tarte of Damsons

Take the damsons and boil them in wine, either red or claret, and put in a dozen pears or else white bread to make them stiff. Mix them with the yolks of six eggs and sweet butter and bake.

### To Make a Tarte of Borage Floures

Take borage flowers and parboil them until tender, then strain them with the yolks of three or four eggs and sweet curds, or else take three or four apples and parboil them and strain them. Add sweet butter and a little mace and bake.

### To Make a Tarte of Marigoldes, Prymroses or Couslips

Take the same mixture as for the borage tart and the same seasoning.

### To Make a Tarte of Strawberyes

Take and strain them with the yolks of four eggs, and a little grated white bread (breadcrumbs). Season with sugar and sweet butter and bake.

The Booke
of damsons, so that ye putte no perys
therto.

¶ To make a tarte of spinage.

Take Spynage and perboyle it tender, then take it vp and wrynge oute the water cleane, and chop it very small, and set it vppon the fyre wyth swete butter in a frying panne, and season it, and set it in a platter to coole, than fyll vp your tart, and so bake it.

¶ To make a tarte of Chese.

Take harde Chese and cutte it in slyces, and pare it, than laye it in fayre water, or in swete mylke, the space of three houres, then take it vp and breake it in a morter, tyll it be small, than drawe it vp thorowe a strainer with the yolkes of syre egges, and season it vp wyth suger and swete butter, and so bake it.

¶ To make a stewe after the guyse of beyonde the Sea.

Take a pottel of fayre water, and as much wyne, and a breste of Mutton chopt in peces, than set it on the fyre, and scome it cleane, than put therto a dysshe full of slyced onyons, and a quantitie of synamō, gynger, cloues and mace, wyth salte, and
stewe

### To Make a Tarte of Cheryes

Make this like the damson tart so that you add no perys (a drink similar to cider) to it.

### To Make a Tarte of Spinage

Take the spinach and parboil until tender. Remove and wring out the water, and chop it very fine. Put it on the heat with some sweet butter in a frying pan and season it. Put it on a plate to cool and then fill the tart and bake.

### To Make a Tarte of Chese

Take hard cheese and cut it into slices, and put it in fresh water or in sweet milk for three hours. Then take it out and break it up in a mortar until it is in small pieces. Strain through a strainer with the yolks of five eggs, season with sugar and sweet butter, and bake.

### To Make a Stewe After the Guyse of Beyonde the Sea

(the foreign fashion)

Take a pottel of fresh water, and the same amount of wine, and a breast of mutton chopped in pieces, then set it on the fire. Take off the scum and put in a dishful of sliced onions, and a quantity of cinnamon, ginger, cloves and mace with salt, and stew all this together and serve on soppes.

Of Cokerye.

stewe them all together, and than serue them wyth soppes.

¶ To make egges in moneshyne.

Take a dyshe of rosewater and a dyshe full of suger, and sette them vpon a chaffyngdysh and let them boyle, than take the yolkes of .viii. or .ix. egges newe layde and putte them therto, euery one from other, and so lette them harden a lytile, and so after this maner serue them forthe, and cast a lytile synamon and suger vpon the.

¶ To make an Applemoyse.

Take a dosen apples, and ether rooste or boyle theim, and drawe them thorowe a streyner, and the yolkes of three or foure egges withal, and as ye strayne theym, tēper them wyth three or foure sponefull of Damaske water yf ye wyll, than take and seaſon it wyth suger, and halfe a dyshe of swete butter, and boyle them vpon a chaffyngdysche in a platter, and caste byskettes or synamō and gynger vpon them, and so serue them forthe.

¶ To frye Trypes.

Take youre Tripes and cutte them in small peces and put them into a panne and put therto an onyon or two, and a

B.iiii.                         by the

## To Make Egges in Moneshyne

(rosewater and spun sugar)

Take a dish of rosewater and a dishful of sugar, and put them on the fire and let them boil. Then take the yolks of eight or nine new-laid eggs, and put them in separately until they harden a little (possibly poached). After this, serve them sprinkled with a little cinnamon and sugar.

## To Make Applemoyse

Take a dozen apples and either roast or boil them and put them through a strainer with the yolks of three or four eggs. As you strain them, mix with three or four spoonfuls of damaske water (rosewater) as much as you like, and season with sugar and half a dish of sweet butter. Boil together in a dish over the heat. Sprinkle biscuits or cinnamon and ginger on them and serve.

The boke

dysshe of swete butter, and let them frye tyll they be browne, and then take them oute and set them vpon a chaffindysh, and put thereto a lyttle verges and gynger, and serue it.

### To make a tarte of Prunes.

Take prunes and set them vpon a chafer wyth a lyttle red wyne, and putte therto a manchet, and let them boyle together, then drawe them thorowe a streyner with the yolkes of foure egges and season it vp wyth suger and so bake it.

### To make a couer tarte after the frenche fasshyon.

Take a pynte of creme and the yolkes of tenne egges, and beate them all together, and put therto halfe a dyshe of swete butter, and suger, and boyle them til they be thicke, then take them vp and coole them in a platter, and make a couple of cakes of fyne paeste, and laye youre stuffe in one of them, and couer it wyth the other and cutte the vente aboue, and so bake it.

### To stewe capons in whyte brothe.

Take foure or fyne biefe bones to make youre brothe, then take them oute when they are sodden and streyne the brothe

into

### To Frye Trypes

Take the tripe and cut into small pieces and put in a pan with an onion or two and a dish of sweet butter. Let the mixture fry until brown, and then take it out and lay the tripe in a heated dish. Sprinkle with a little verges and ginger and serve.

### To Make a Tarte of Prunes

Take the prunes and put them in a pan over the heat with a little red wine and a manshet (a small white loaf) and let them boil together. Then strain them through a strainer with the yolks of four eggs and season with sugar and bake.

### To Make a Couer Tarte After the Frenche Fashyan

(This is shaped like a huge mince pie covered with pastry and filled with custard.)

Take a pint of cream and the yolks of ten eggs, and beat them all together. Add half a dish (cup) of sweet butter, and sugar, and boil until thickened. Then take it out and cool it on a plate. Make a couple of cakes of fine pastry, and lay the mixture on one and cover with the other, then cut out the vent (the hole for the steam) and bake.

## Of cokerye.

into another potte, then putte in youre capons hole wyth rosemarye and putte them into the pot, and let them stewe, and after they haue boyled a whyle, putte in hole Mace bounde in a whyte clothe, and a handefull or twayne of hole perselye and hole prunes, and lette them boyle well, and at the takyng vp put to a lytile vergis, and salte, and so strawe them vpon soppes and the marybones aboute and the marrowe layde hole aboue them, and so serue them forth.

### ¶ For Gusset that maye be another potage.

Take the broathe of the same Capons and putte in a fayre chafer, then take a doosen or syrtene egges and stere them all together whyte and all, then grate a farthynge whyte loafe as smale as ye canne, and mynce it wyth the egges all togeather, and putte thereto salte and a good quantite of safiron, and or ye putte in youre egges, putte into youre brothe, tyme, sauerye, margeron, and parsely small chopped, and when ye are redye to your dynner, sette the chafer vppon the fyre wyth the broihe, and lette it boyle a lytile and putte in youre egges

B.y.

## To Stewe Capons in Whyte Brothe

Take four or five beef bones to make the broth and take them out when they are sodden, and strain the broth into another pot. Then put the capons whole into the pot with rosemary and let them stew. After they have boiled for a while, put in whole mace bound in a white cloth, a handful or two of whole parsley and whole prunes, and let them boil well. When serving put in a little verges and salt, and lay them on the soppes with the marrow bones around them and the whole marrow on top, and serve.

## For Gusset That Maye be Another Potage

(Gusset was broth without meat.)

Take the broth of the capons and put it in a pan over the heat. Then take a dozen or sixteen eggs and stir them all together, whites and all, and grate a farthing white loaf as small as you can, and mix with the eggs. Add salt and a good quantity of saffron and then, before adding the eggs, put into the broth, thyme, savory, marjoram, and parsley chopped small. When ready to eat, put the pan with the broth on the fire and add the eggs, stirring well to prevent curdling. The less it is boiled, the more tender it will be. Then serve it in two or three slices on a dish.

#### The Booke

ges, and stere it vp well for quaylynge the lesse, The lesse boylynge it hathe the more tender it wyll be, and then serue it forthe, two or three slyces vpon a dysshe.

#### ⁋ To make a whyte broathe.

Take a necke of mutton and fayre water, and sette it vpon the fyre and scome it cleane, and lette it boyle halfe awaye, then take forthe of the broathe two ladlefull, and put them in a platter, then chop two handefuls of parsely not to small, and let it boile with the mutton, then take twelue egges, and the sayde two ladle fuls of broathe and vergis, so that it be tarte of the vergis, and streyne them all together, then season your broathe with salte, and a lyttle before you goo to diner, put al these to your mutton, and stere it well for qualling, and serue it forth wyth soppes.

#### ⁋ Another broath with longe wortes.

Take mutton and fayre water, and let them boyle vpō the fyre, and then take lettuse or spynage, and put therto, and yf ye lyst to boile therwith two or thre chekins, and put therto salt and vergis after your discretion, and serue them forth, the flesh vnder,

## To Make a Whyte Broathe

Take a neck of mutton and fresh water, put it over the heat and skim it clean (remove the scum). Let it boil half away (reduce the volume by half), then remove two ladlefuls of the broth and save. Then chop two handfuls of parsley, not too finely, and let boil with the mutton. Then add twelve eggs to the two ladlefuls of broth, and add verges to taste, not letting it become too tart, and strain them together. Season the broth with salt and just before eating add this mixture to the mutton, stirring carefully to prevent curdling, and serve on soppes.

## Another Broath with Longewortes

(This would have been a vegetable broth, usually made with cabbage, but here using lettuce and spinach.)

Take mutton and fresh water, and let it boil over the heat. Then take lettuce or spinach, and put it in, and if you like boil two or three chickens with it. Add salt and verges to taste, and serve with the meat under and the herbs over it.

Of cokerye,
vnder, the herbes aboue.

¶ To make a Frasye at nyght.

Take chekins heades, lyuers, gyber﹀
nes, wynges, feete, and chop them in peces
of helfe an ynche longe, and boyle them al
together, and when the broath is almoste
soden away, chop a lyttle parsely, and put
therto with vergis, & halfe a dysshe of but﹀
ter, and so lette them boyle, and let it be
tart ynoughe, and so serue it in.

¶ To make Shoes.

Take a rumpe of beyfe and let it boyle
an houre or two, and put therto a greate
quantitye of cole wortes, and lette them
boyle together thre houres, then putte to
them a couple of stockedoues, or teales, fe﹀
sande, partriche, or suche other wylde fou﹀
les, and let them boyle al together, then
ceason them wyth salte, and serue them
forthe.

¶ To make Porape.

Take a Capon or a hen, and eyther beyf or
mutton to make the broath swete withal,
and boyle theym all together tyll they be
very tender, then take the capon or hen oute
of the pot, & take out al his bones & braye
hym in a morter, wyth .ii. pounde of almõdes
ouer﹀

## To Make a Frasye at Nyght

(Frayse usually means something fried or frittered.)

Take chicken heads, livers, gizzards, wings and feet, and chop them in pieces half an inch long, and boil all them all together. When they are almost boiled away, chop a little parsley, and add this with verges and half a dish of butter. Let it boil until tart enough and serve.

## To Make Shoes

(Shoes is a name for stew.)

Take a rump of beef and boil it for an hour or two, and put in a large amount of cole wortes (cabbage, powdered and salted) and let it boil for three hours more. Then add a couple of wild or wood pigeons or teals, pheasants, partridges or such other wild fowls, and boil them together. Season with salt and serve.

## To Make Porraye

(Purée)

Take a capon or a hen, and either beef or mutton to make the broth sweet, and boil them all together till they are very tender. Then take the capon or hen out of the pot, take out the bones and pound in a mortar with a pound of blanched almonds, then with the broth of the capon or hen, strain until appropriately thick and then put into a little pot. Season with a little sugar, saunders (a saffron-like colouring), cloves, mace and small raisins and boil together. Serve on soppes.

The Booke.

ouerblaunced, then wyth the broathe of youre Capon or Henne, strayne them metely thicke, then putte it into a lyttle potte, and ceason it wyth a lyttle suger, sanders, cloues, mace, and small reysons, so boyle hym, and serue hym vpon soppes,

¶ To stewe bones or gristels of biefe.

Take gristels of beyfe, and stewe them as tender as ye canne, fyre houres so that there be no broathe lefte that shall serue you as that tyme, then putte a good boundell of rosemarye in a fayre lynnen clothe, and a good quantite of mace in another clothe, and boyle them all together, then wrynge oute the iuyce of the rosemarye, and mace vppon the fleshe, and ceason it wyth salte, and so serue hym.

¶ For to stewe Mutton.

Take a necke of mutton and a breste to make the brothe stronge, and the scome it clene, and when it hath boyled a whyle take part of the brathe, and putte it in to another pot and put therto a pounde of reysons, and let them boyle tyll they be tender, then strayne a litle bread wyth the reysons and the broth all together, then chop tyme, sauery, and persely wyth other

Smal

### To Stewe Bones or Gristels of Biefe

Take the gristle of beef and stew until as tender as you can, for six hours so that there is little broth left. Then put in a good bundle of rosemary in a cloth and mace in another cloth and boil together (to make the gravy). Strain the rosemary juice with mace on to the meat. Season with salt and serve.

### For to Stewe Mutton

Take a neck and a breast of mutton to make a strong broth and skim it clean. After it has boiled for a while, take out some of the broth and put it into another pot with a pound of raisins and boil until tender. Then strain a little bread with the raisins and the broth and chop thyme, savory and parsley with the other small herbs. Add these to the mutton and then put in the raisins and whole prunes, cloves and mace, pepper, saffron and a little salt. If you like, you may also stew a chicken or else a sparrow or such other little birds.

### Of Cokerye.

small herbes, and putte into the mutton then, putte in the streyned reysins wyth whole prunes, cloues, and mace, peper, saffron, and a lytle salte, and yf ye lyste ye maye item a chikin withal or els sparowes or suche other lytle byrdes.

### To stewe stekes of mutton.

Take a legge of mutton, and cot it in small slices, and put it in a chafer, and put therto a pottel of ale, and scome it cleane then putte therto seuen or eyghte onions thyn slyced, and after they haue boyled one houre, putte thereto a dyshe of swete butter, and so lette them boyle tyll they be tender, and then put therto a lytle peper and salte.

### ¶ For to make wardens in conserue.

Fyrste make the syrope in this wyse, take a quarte of good romney, and put te a pynte of clarysyed honey, a pounde or a halfe of suger, and myngle all those together ouer the fyre, tyll tyme they seeth, and then set it to cole. And thys is a good sirope for manye thinges, and wyll be kepte a yeare or two. Then take thy warden and scrape cleane awaye the barke, but pare them not, and seeth them in good redde wyne so that they be

## To Stewe Stekes of Mutton

Take a leg of mutton and cut it into small slices. Put it in a pan over heat, and add a pottell of ale and skim it clean. Then put in seven or eight onions thinly sliced, and after they have boiled for one hour add a dish (cup) of sweet butter and boil until tender. Then add a little pepper and salt.

## For to Make Wardens in Conserue

(Wardens were large baking pears.)

First make the syrup this way. Take a quart of Romney (wine) and add a pint of clear honey, and a pound and a half of sugar, and stir all together over the heat till ready and then leave to cool. This is a good syrup for many things and will keep a year or two. Then take the wardens and skin, but do not pare, and simmer them in good red wine so that they are well soaked and tender, and the wine is well soaked in to them. Then strain through a cloth or through a strainer into a vessel, adding the syrup until the vessel is almost full. Then add the powdered spices such as fine canel (a cinnamon-like spice), cinnamon, ginger and others. Put in boxes and keep as long as you like. By experience the correct amount for twenty or so wardens can be made.

The Boke of Cokerye.
bewel foked and tender, that the wyne be
nere háde foked into them, then take and
ſtrayne them throughe a cloth or through
a ſtrayner into a veſſell, then put to them
of this ſyrope aforeſayde tyll it be almoſt
fylled, and then caſte in the pouders, as
fyne canel, ſynamon, pouder of gynger,
and ſuch other, & put it in a bores, and
kepe it yf thou wylt, and make thy
Syrope as thou wylt worke in
quantyte, as yf thou wylt
worke twenty wardens
or more, or leſſe, as
by experience.

# FINIS.

¶ Imprynted at London, in
Crede Lane, by John
Kynge, and Tho-
mas Marche.

# 𝔉𝔍𝔑𝔍𝔖

Imprinted at London in Crede
Lane, by John Kinge and
Thomas Marche

# Recipes

Modern cooks may wish to try the recipes in Margaret Parker's cookery book. In this section some of them have been adapted in an informal manner to make sixteenth-century dishes available to twenty-first-century cooks. Ingredients and method are supplied, and cross-references direct the reader to the original recipe. Readers may wish to try out their own variations.

## To Stewe Capons in Whyte Brothe
(See page 71)

*Ingredients*
1 small free-range chicken or 4 skinned chicken breasts
1 oz (25g) butter
2 onions
A glass of white wine
A beef-stock cube
2 oz (50g) currants
6 ready-to-eat prunes
6 pitted dates
4 egg yolks
Half a teaspoon rosewater
Half a teaspoon ground mace
Bouquet garni consisting of thyme, rosemary, marjoram, parsley and chicory
Salt and pepper
Slices of brown bread with crusts removed

*Method*

Skin the chicken or use skinned chicken breasts. Brown the chicken in the melted butter with the onions in a heavy-based pan. When the chicken is brown, add a glass of white wine. Add stock made with a beef-stock cube, enough to come half way up the chicken.

Add salt and pepper to taste together with the mace. Put in the bouquet garni, tied in a muslin cloth. Boil for about forty minutes until the chicken is tender, turning it once or twice in the pan. (If you use chicken breasts, these will need a much shorter time, about ten to fifteen minutes.)

About ten minutes before it is ready, add the prunes, currants and dates tied in a cloth.

When the chicken is ready, take it out of the pan and keep it warm.

Remove the two muslin parcels.

Reduce the stock by about one half until you have about one pint of liquid.

Beat the egg yolks with the rosewater and add slowly to the stock, heating gently but not allowing it to boil, to avoid curdling. Then pour it over the chicken.

Decorate with the fruit and serve over the bread.

Other recipes in the book have used eggs for thickening the broth and this method has been used here.

# To Make a Pye of Alowes
(See page 59)

*Ingredients*

12 oz (300g) short-crust pastry (see recipe page 93)
1½ lb (675g) leg of lamb sliced thinly
6 hard-boiled egg yolks
6 oz (150g) raisins
6 oz (150g) chopped dates
Plenty of parsley and thyme
Half a teaspoon mace
Half a teaspoon ginger
Half a teaspoon cinnamon
2 teaspoons sugar
Salt to taste
10 oz (250ml) red wine
Breadcrumbs made from
2 slices of white bread

*Method*

Take about two-thirds of the pastry, roll it out and cover the base and sides of a buttered pie dish.

Flatten the lamb slices with a rolling pin.

Place the lamb slices in layers in the pie, interspersed with the egg yolks, dates, raisins, parsley and thyme.

Warm the wine to boiling point and then add to it the breadcrumbs, salt, mace, ginger, cinnamon and sugar. Pour this into the pie.

Place a pie funnel firmly in the middle of the pie on the pastry base.

Cover with the remaining pastry, making a hole for the pie funnel. Make a few extra holes in the pastry lid.

Glaze the top with egg yolk or milk.

Bake in a preheated oven (150–160°C) for about forty-five minutes.

The original recipe in *A Proper Newe Booke of Cokerye* states that the meat should be rolled up over the egg yolks and herbs, and that the sauce should be added just before serving.

## To Make a Tarte of Chese
(See page 65)

*Ingredients*

8 oz (200g) short-crust pastry (see recipe page 93)
6 oz (150g) Cheddar cheese
6 egg yolks
1 oz (25g) caster sugar
1 oz (25g) unsalted butter

*Method*

Line a flan dish with the pastry and bake blind for seven to ten minutes in a preheated oven (200°C).

Grate the cheese and mix with the egg yolks, sugar and butter in a food processor until smooth.

Bake in the oven for a further thirty minutes until set and golden brown.

## To Stewe Stekes of Mutton
(See page 79)

*Ingredients*
2 lb (approximately 1kg) cubed leg of lamb
1 pint of Guinness
2 large onions, sliced
Salt and pepper to taste
2 oz (50g) butter
3 slices of brown bread, cubed and
with crusts removed

*Method*
Place the meat and onions and pour
the Guinness into a casserole. Simmer
on the hob for one hour until the
meat is tender.
Add salt and pepper to taste.
Add the butter and stir.
Place the cubed bread in
a deep serving dish.
Pour the stew over
and serve.

# To Make Applemoyse

(See page 67)

*Ingredients*

1½ lb (675g) of cooking apples (peeled, cored and sliced)
6 tablespoons water
2 egg yolks
2 tablespoons rosewater
3 tablespoons sugar
1 oz (25ml) water
Ground ginger and cinnamon

*Method*

Place the apples with the water into a heavy-based saucepan and cook until soft, stirring frequently to prevent sticking.

Strain the apples through a sieve.

Add the egg yolks, rosewater, butter and sugar to the apple mixture.

Return the mixture to the saucepan and heat gently, stirring constantly.

Spoon into dishes.

Sprinkle with a mixture of ground cinnamon and ginger.

# To Make a Custarde
(See page 47)

*Ingredients*
6 oz (150g) short-crust pastry (see recipe page 93)
10 oz (250ml) double cream
4 egg yolks
2 oz (50g) sugar
4 oz (100g) ground almonds
1 oz (25g) chopped dates
1 oz (25g) raisins
1 teaspoon rosewater
Half a teaspoon cinnamon
Half a teaspoon ginger

*Method*
Grease a flan dish and line with the pastry, weighting it with baking parchment held down by beans. Bake the pastry blind in a preheated oven (180–200°C) for about ten minutes.
Warm the cream with the ground almonds. Beat up the egg yolks and add them slowly. Add the remaining ingredients. Pour into the pastry case and continue to bake at the same temperature for about another twenty minutes, until set and slightly browned.

## Short-crust pastry

*Ingredients*
6 oz (150g) plain flour
3 oz (75g) unsalted butter
Pinch of salt
Cold water to mix

*Method*
Measure out the flour.
Add the salt and rub in the butter.
Add water and mix until the dough is stiff but moist.
Cover and chill.

(This recipe is used
for short-crust pastry
throughout this section.)

## To Make a Dyshefull of Snowe
(See page 49)

*Ingredients*
4 large egg whites
8 oz (200g) sugar
2 tablespoons rosewater
4 oz (100ml) double cream
2 lb (approximately 1kg) eating apples; cooking apples may be used for a tarter taste
A small sprig of rosemary
Ratafia biscuits or wafers

*Method*
Peel, core and slice the apples and cook them gently in the rosewater, adding a little water if necessary, until they are soft.
Strain through a sieve, or use an electric blender. (These methods will result in different textures.)
Beat the egg whites and add the sugar, to form a stiff mixture.
Fold in the apple mixture.
Decorate with whipped cream and rosemary and serve with the wafers.

# For to Make Wardens in Conserve
(See page 81)
(Wardens were large cooking pears.)

*Ingredients*
10 oz (250ml) of good red wine
5 oz (125ml) clear honey (orange-blossom honey was used)
4 oz (100g) sugar
1 cinnamon stick
1 teaspoon ground ginger
Zest of 1 lemon
4 large pears

*Method*
Heat all the ingredients except the pears slowly together to boiling point, stirring constantly.
Skin the pears, leaving them whole.
Add the pears to the syrup and simmer slowly until they are tender.
Lay the pears in a dish, surrounding them with the syrup.

This dish proved to be both delicious and simple.

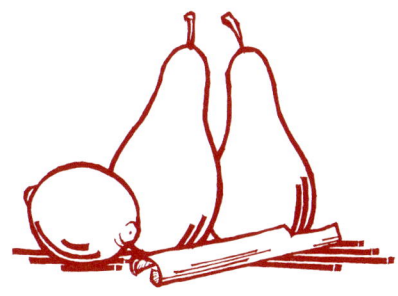

# Bibliography

Brears, P. Tudor Britain, in *A Taste of History: 10,000 Years of Food in Britain*, by P. Brears *et al.* (London, 1997)

Bury, P. *The College of Corpus Christi and of the Blessed Virgin Mary: a History from 1822 to 1952*. Reissue (Woodbridge, 1995)

Durant, D.N. *Bess of Hardwick: Portrait of an Elizabethan Dynast*. Revised ed. (London, 1999)

Frere, C.F., ed. *A Proper Newe Booke of Cokerye* (Cambridge, 1913)

Lamb, J., ed. *Masters' History of the College of Corpus Christi and the Blessed Virgin Mary in the University of Cambridge* (Cambridge, 1831)

Perry, E.W. *Under Four Tudors, Being the Story of Matthew Parker Sometime Archbishop of Canterbury*. 2nd ed. (London, 1964)

Rupp, G. *Matthew Parker, a Man* (Cambridge, 1975)

Sim, A. *The Tudor Housewife*. Repr. (Stroud, 2000)

Spurling, H. *Elinor Fettiplace's Receipt Book: Elizabethan Country House Cooking* (London, 1986)

Stokes, H.P. *Corpus Christi* (University of Cambridge college histories) (London, 1898)

Strype, J. *The Life and Acts of Matthew Parker...* (London, 1711)